The Skating Twins

Story by Annette Smith and Jenny Giles
Illustrations by Genevieve Rees

"I'll race you back to our place,"
said Nick to his sister, Sarah.

He sped off down the path
on his skates.
As he raced along, he looked back
to see where Sarah was.

Suddenly, Nick lost his balance
and fell into Mrs. Miller's garden.

Sarah started to laugh.
"Look what you did
to Mrs. Miller's flowers!" she said.

"Help!" said Nick. "Here she comes."

"And here comes Dad, too," said Sarah.

4

"Sorry, Mrs. Miller," said Nick.
"I didn't mean to run over your flowers."

"No more skating out here,"
said Dad. "Come on.
We'll go to the park
and you can skate there."

When they arrived at the park,
Sarah and Nick ran across the grass
to a big wide path.
They were just about
to put on their in-line skates
when Dad said,
"Look! You can't skate here either!"

Sarah and Nick were very disappointed.

"It's not fair," groaned Sarah.
"Where can we go?"

"Well, I think we'd better forget
about skating today,"
answered Dad.
"I'll take you to the beach instead."

"There are too many flowers
here anyway," said Nick.

NO SKATING in this park

As Dad drove along the road
by the beach, Sarah noticed
some people on in-line skates.

"Hey, Dad," she cried,
"there's a path
for in-line skating here.
It seems to go all the way
along the beachfront."

Dad parked the car
and the twins put on their skates.
They sat on the beach wall
and watched all the people going past.

"Look at that man," laughed Dad,
as he sat down beside them.
"He's found a good way
to exercise his dog."

"And people are skating
with their kids, too," said Nick.

"Dad, could you take us?" asked Sarah.

"Well," said Dad, "I used to go skating when I was your age,
but I didn't have in-line skates like yours.
I don't know if I could even
stand up in those things."

"Yes, you could," said Nick. "It's easy."

"You can rent in-line skates
from that shop over there," said Sarah.

"Go on, Dad," said Nick.

"All right, I'll give it a try,"
grinned Dad.

IN-LINE
SKATES
FOR
RENT

11

Sarah and Nick helped Dad
as he wobbled about on the in-line skates.

"Don't go too fast, or I'll fall over,"
Dad laughed.

Everyone sped past them.
"Move over!" someone shouted at Dad.

Sarah and Nick were a bit embarrassed.

Dad hobbled off the path
and rested against a tree.
"You two can go on ahead," he puffed,
"but please don't go too far.
It's important that I keep you in sight."

The twins raced off together.

"This is fun," said Sarah.
"I really like skating along here."

"But we'd better get back to Dad, now,"
said Nick.

"Look, Nick!" shouted Sarah,
as she spun around.
"Here comes Dad on his skates!"

"I'm nearly as good as you two, now,"
said Dad, when he came alongside them.
"There's nothing like a bit of practice."

"We've found the perfect place
to skate," said Sarah.

"Yes," grinned Nick,
"and there are no flowers here either!"